b small publishing

D053 3000

DINOSAUR DISHES

AND

FOSSIL

FOOD

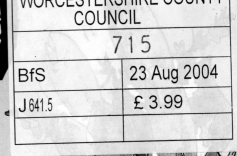

Susan Martineau

Illustrations by Martin Ursell

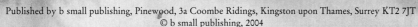

Published by b small publishing, Pinewood, 3a Coombe Ridings, Kingston upon Thames, Surrey KT2 7JT

© b small publishing, 2004

5 4 3 2 1

Colour reproduction: Vimnice International Ltd., Hong Kong.   Printed in China by WKT Company Ltd.

Editorial: Susan Martineau and Sally Wood *Design:* Louise Millar *Production:* Madeleine Ehm

ISBN 1 902915 06 2

British Library Cataloguing-in-Publication Data. A catalogue record for this book is available from the British Library.

Before You Begin

You'll really impress your friends with these prehistoric dishes. They're great for dinosaur parties and fun for lunch-boxes too.

When you've chosen a recipe, read it all the way through and get all of the ingredients and equipment ready before starting to cook. Wash your hands first and remember to tidy up nicely afterwards! All the recipes will serve four children unless it says otherwise.

It's a good idea to have an adult standing by when you are using the oven or cutting with sharp knives.

Always keep some oven gloves handy, too, for handling hot pans and tins.

Don't forget that these recipes are just to get you started – you can make up all sorts of fossil food yourself.

3

Dino Hatchlings

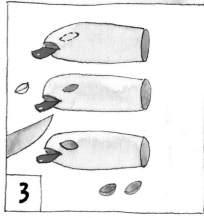

These poor little dinos may never make it.
A large, carnivorous beast is going to eat them – you!

What you will need:
- 4 large potatoes, scrubbed clean
- 2 frankfurters, cut in half
- tomato ketchup

- mayonnaise or salad cream
- small pieces of red and green pepper

Prick the potatoes with a fork.

1

Bake the potatoes in the oven at 200°C/400°F/Gas 6 for 1–1½ hours. When they are cooked they will feel soft when squeezed.

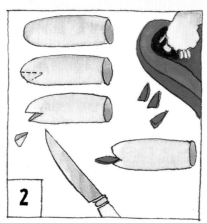

2

Cut a wedge out of each rounded frankfurter end to make a mouth. Cut small triangles of red pepper and push inside for a tongue.

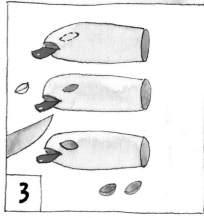

3

Cut tiny slits on each side of the mouth. Cut out slivers of green pepper and push into the slits for eyes.

Cut a cross in each potato.

4

Open the potatoes up slightly. Place a dollop of mayonnaise and some ketchup inside.

5

Push a frankfurter into each potato so that it is standing up. Nestle on a bed of salad leaves.

Egg Stealers

Oviraptors were egg thieves. That's what their name means. They were quite small dinosaurs but they could run fast and had great big front claws for grabbing eggs. Then they used their bony beaks to break them open.

5

Plesiosaur's Pond

This is a warming swampy soup complete with prehistoric foliage. The Fossil Fodder on page 12 is pretty tasty with this.

What you will need for 4 small servings or 2 large ones:

- 1 tablespoon vegetable or olive oil
- 1 medium-sized onion, chopped small
- 2 leeks, washed and chopped
- 25 g red lentils
- 75 g split green peas
- 1 litre vegetable stock
- pinch of dried thyme
- salt and pepper
- fresh parsley sprigs
- celery stalks with leaves on

1 Heat the oil in a large saucepan. Add the onion and leeks. Cook gently until they are soft.

2 Add the lentils, peas, stock and thyme. Simmer for 1 hour with the lid half on until the peas are soft.

3 Add salt and pepper to taste. Roughly liquidize the mixture in a blender or food processor.

4 Serve the soup in bowls. Stand parsley and celery stalks around the edges.

Monster in the Lake

Plesiosaurs were long-necked reptiles that fed on fish and other reptiles. Some people think that the legendary Loch Ness Monster in Scotland is a plesiosaur trapped in the loch when the level of the seas went down millions of years ago. Maybe there's more than one!

Pterosaur Wings

These make a delicious snack or great party nibble for a bunch of meat-eaters.

What you will need:
- 8 chicken wings
- 3 tablespoons maple syrup
- grated zest of half an orange
- 1 tablespoon soy sauce

1

Mix together the syrup, zest and soy sauce in a small bowl.

2

Place the wings on a roasting tray. Pour the sauce over them.

Turn them in the sauce once or twice.

3

Put them in the oven at 190°C/375°F/Gas 5 for about 25 minutes until nicely browned.

Flying Dinos

Pterosaurs were beautiful great flying reptiles.
Although they could fly they were not related to birds.
Some of them were really enormous.
Quetzalcoatlus (bet you can't say that!) had a wingspan
of about 12 metres. That's bigger than a hang glider.

T. rex Ribs

Get your teeth into these juicy bones. They are a carnivore's feast and brilliant for parties and lunch-boxes.

What you will need:

- 450 g pork spare ribs
- splash of vegetable or olive oil
- 1 small onion, finely chopped
- 1 garlic clove, peeled and finely chopped
- 1 tablespoon soy sauce
- 1 tablespoon runny honey
- 1½ tablespoons tomato purée
- 1 teaspoon Worcestershire sauce

1

Heat the oil in a small saucepan and fry the onion and garlic gently until softened.

2

Remove from the heat. Add all the other ingredients except the ribs. Mix thoroughly.

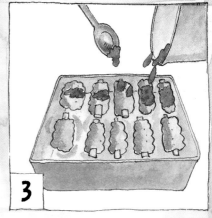

3

Put the ribs in a roasting tin and smother with the sauce mix.

4

Roast the ribs in the oven at 200°C/400°F/Gas 6 for 1–1¼ hours. Turn them around in the sauce from time to time.

King of the Dinos

There's no doubt that Tyrannosaurus rex was a real terror! He had huge jaws strong enough to crush bones and a mouth big enough to swallow you whole. His teeth were as long as the knife you use to eat your dinner.

T. rex's eyes faced forwards so that he was very good at spotting prey. He was about 15 metres long and as tall as a two-storey house. You'd definitely have heard him coming!

Dino Dung

Make some delicious droppings for all your friends to enjoy!

What you will need to make about 10 lumps:

- 225 g self-raising flour
- pinch of salt
- 75 g butter or margarine, cut into pieces
- 100 g plain chocolate
- 75 g caster sugar
- 1 egg, beaten
- 2 tablespoons milk

Use only your fingertips and thumbs.

1

The mixture will be quite thick.

2

Bake until light brown.

3

Sieve the flour and salt into a large bowl. Add the butter or margarine and rub it into the flour.

Cut the chocolate into small chunks. Mix it into the flour with the sugar. Add the egg and milk.

Plonk piles of the mixture on to a greased baking tray. Bake in the oven at 180°C/350°F/Gas 4 for about 15 minutes.

Place the dung on a cooling rack.

4

Ask a grown-up to help you take the tray out of the oven. You could serve the droppings on a bed of green liquorice 'grasses'.

Excremental Evidence

Fossilized dinosaur droppings have a proper scientific name – coprolites. It's not surprising that most of them were pretty big! Amazingly, scientists can get an idea of what dinosaurs ate from examining this petrified poo.

Flies in Amber

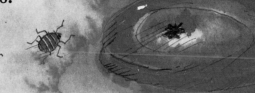

Preserve some flies in your own version of prehistoric amber. You need to use very small containers – eggcups are ideal – to make these. (Remember with half a pack of jelly you only need half the amount of water it says on the pack.)

What you will need to make about 8:
- ½ pack orange jelly
- handful of raisins
- jug and spoon

1

Make the jelly in a jug following the instructions on the packet.

2

Allow it to cool down completely. Snip some raisins with scissors to make them 'fray' a bit.

3

Pour some jelly mixture into 8 eggcups or small bowls. Pop 1 or 2 raisins into each. Put them in the fridge to set.

4

Dip each eggcup or bowl into warm water to loosen the jellies and turn them out on to plates.

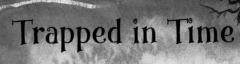

Trapped in Time

Amber is the fossilized sap of trees. Many types of insect are found preserved in amber. They would have been trapped in the sap while it was still runny, millions of years ago. Some of the insects are so well preserved that you can clearly see the lacework of their wings and their colour patterns. Amazing!

Fossil Fodder

Challenge your friends to fit these bones together to make part of a dino skeleton. They are delicious eaten with the Plesiosaur's Pond on page 6. Try making up your own remains – a jawbone, maybe, or some fossil feet and claws.

What you will need:

- 100 g plain flour plus extra for dusting
- 75 g finely grated Cheddar cheese
- pinch of paprika or cayenne pepper
- salt and pepper
- 50 g butter or margarine
- 1 egg yolk

1 Mix the flour with the cheese, salt and both peppers. Rub in the butter or margarine, using your thumbs and fingertips.

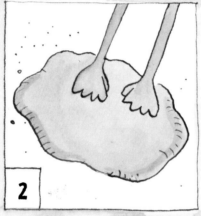

2 Mix in the egg yolk and form the mixture into a ball of dough. Knead it a little bit.

3 Dust your work-top with flour. Roll the dough out until it is about ¹/₂ cm thick.

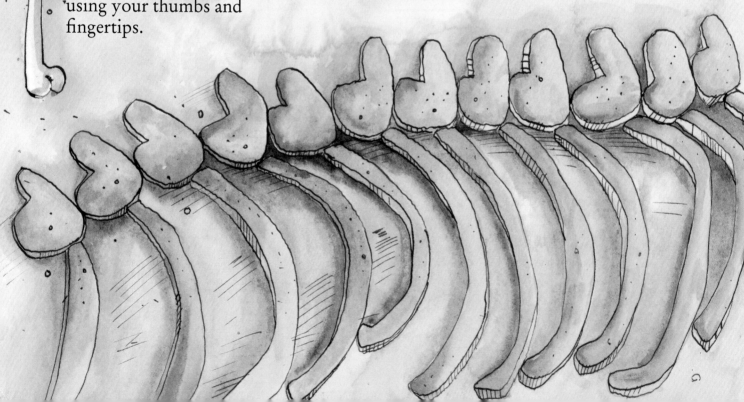

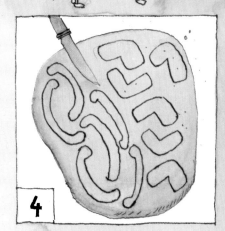

4 Cut out backbones and rib shapes as shown. Use a knife to carve them out.

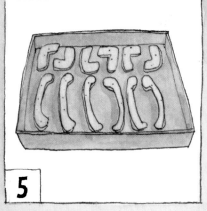

5 Make as many as you like and place them on an UNGREASED baking tray. Bake in the oven at 180°C/350°F/Gas 4 for 15 minutes.

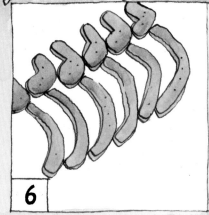

6 Cool on a rack and then piece the backbones and ribs together.

Ammonite Whirls

Use up the off-cuts of dough to make these fossils. Roll the dough into sausages. Curl them up. Flatten slightly and score with a knife and bake for 20 minutes as above.

Dinosaur Detectives

Fossilized bones are the main evidence we have that dinosaurs even existed. Scientists have to use clever ways to work out what the dinosaurs would have looked like when they were alive. The bones have rough marks on them and these show scientists where the muscles were attached and where blood vessels may have been.

Fossil impressions of dinosaur skin have also been found and this helps fossil-hunters to know if a dinosaur was covered in scales or knobbly skin. Gradually the evidence is pieced together like a prehistoric detective story.

Ice Age Bowl

This is a fantastic centrepiece for any dinosaur party. You can serve all kinds of things in it – Glacial Deposits (see page 15) or Flies in Amber (page 11). Just don't eat the bowl! There are some great fossil-like pasta shapes in the shops. Use bowls with a gap between them of about 2–3 cm when the little one is inside the medium one.

What you will need:

- 4–5 handfuls of uncooked dried pasta shapes
- 1 medium freezer-proof bowl
- 1 small freezer-proof bowl
- about 16 ice cubes
- plastic bag and rolling-pin
- sticky tape

1 Put the ice cubes in a plastic bag and bash lightly with a rolling-pin until they are crushed.

2 Fill the gap with more water.

Put the crushed ice into the medium bowl. Add some cold water and float the smaller bowl inside it.

3 Slide handfuls of pasta into the gap between the bowls. Spread them out evenly on the sides and underneath.

4 Let the small bowl float and hold it steady.

Put some pieces of tape across the bowls to keep the rims level with each other. Put the bowls in the freezer for the night.

5 Take off the tape. Put some warm water into the small bowl and lift it out. Dip the medium bowl into hot water and the ice bowl will slip out.

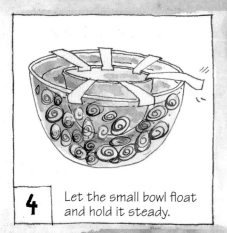

6 Pop the ice bowl into a large plastic bag and keep it in the freezer until it is needed. It can be used over and over again as long as it is put back in the freezer.

Glacial Deposits

These crunchy, icy remains look great served up in the Ice Age Bowl. Just break up some chocolate biscuits and wafer biscuits in a bowl. Add some spoonfuls of soft-scoop vanilla ice-cream and mix.

The Big Freeze?

How did the dinosaurs die out? Some scientists think that a massive meteorite may have crashed into our planet and caused such a large explosion that the dust and debris cut out all the sunlight. This meant that plants could not grow and so the plant-eating dinosaurs died out. The meat-eaters would have had no chance of survival either without their usual prey.

Primordial Sludge

A slime from the mists of time. This tastes a lot better than any algae would! You could serve it in the Ice Age Bowl on page 14.

What you will need:

- 900 g cooking apples, peeled and cored
- 100 g caster sugar
- 300 ml water
- 1 packet lime jelly, broken into pieces

Stir to dissolve the sugar.

1

Slice the apples. Put the sugar and water into a large saucepan and heat it gently.

Stir well to dissolve the jelly.

2

Add the sliced apples. Cover the pan and simmer until they are soft. Turn the heat down. Add the jelly. Mash the apples and jelly together.

3

Pour into a bowl and let the mixture cool. Chill until ready to serve.

Ancient Algae

In Shark Bay in Western Australia living 'rocks', called Stromatolites, can be found by the sea. They consist of layers of single cells of algae which are living examples of the oldest forms of life on earth. The fossilized Stromatolites that have been found in rocks in other places are thought to be more than 3500 million years old.

Trilobite Bites

These yummy chunky bites are full of fossils.

To make about 12 bites:

- 100 g butter or margarine
- 2 tablespoons golden syrup
- 100 g soft brown sugar
- 225 g porridge oats

- pinch of salt
- ½ teaspoon ground cinnamon
- 50 g whole pecan nuts

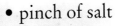

NUT ALLERGY WARNING!

1

Melt the butter or margarine with the syrup and sugar in a pan. Remove from the heat and stir in the oats, salt and cinnamon.

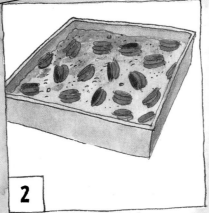

2

Tip into a 16-cm square tin and spread out evenly. Push pecans all over the surface of the mixture.

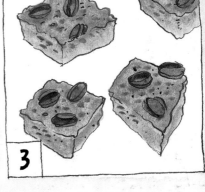

3

Bake at 170°C/325°F/Gas 3 for 20–25 minutes. Leave to cool in the tin. Cut into chunks.

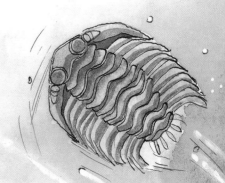

Mud Grovellers

Trilobites are the fossil relations of crabs and crayfish. Their name means 'three-lobed' and you can clearly see the three parts of them in their fossils. Their eyes had many small lenses – just like a fly's. From the fossilized trails they have left in the mud, scientists have been able to tell that they lived and hunted for food on the seabed.

Dead Dinos

These poor Triceratops are dead delicious. You can use the basic burger mix to create other types of horned or spiky dinosaurs too. Try out different garnishes and see what you can come up with.

What you will need to make 4 bodies:
- 450 g lean minced beef
- 1 small onion, very finely chopped
- 1 teaspoon mustard
- 1 teaspoon dried mixed herbs
- salt and pepper

What you will need for the armour:
- 4 thin slices of cucumber
- 4 small 'cocktail' gherkins
- mixed salad leaves
- 12 Bombay mix sticks
- tomato ketchup

First make your bodies:

1 Mix all the body ingredients really well in a bowl. Shape the mixture into 4 body-shaped and head-shaped blobs as shown.

2 Put them under a hot grill for 8–10 minutes. Turn once.

Prepare the dinos' armour:

1 Cut a 'frill' out of each cucumber slice.

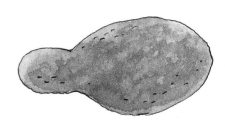

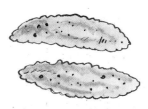

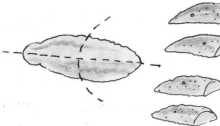

2 Cut each gherkin into four.

3 Put some salad leaves on each plate.

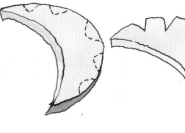

When the bodies are cooked, put 4 gherkin legs underneath each one, and place them on the leaves.

Push 3 sticks into each head as shown.
Make a cut in each neck and insert the cucumber 'frills'.
Dribble ketchup down one side of each Triceratops and tuck in!

Carrot for Stegosaurus plates!

Fancy Frills and Shoulder Spikes

By the end of the time of the dinosaurs, some plant-eaters had developed amazing armour against the fierce attacks of the meat-eaters. Triceratops not only had a huge neck frill but also three horns to fend off predators. Sauropelta had bony studs all over its back and spikes sticking out of its sides. Stegosaurus had a double row of pointed plates on its back.

19

Fossil-hunter's Lunch

These are ideal recipes for a palaeontologist. You could always add some Gastroliths from page 24 just in case you get indigestion.

Jurassic Juice

A refreshing drink for all fossil-hunters. You could try out other combinations of fruits too.

For each person you will need:

- a ripe kiwi fruit
- half a large banana or a whole small one
- ½ glass of apple juice
- a stick of celery with leaves on

1 Peel the kiwi fruit and banana and chop them into chunks. Put them into a food processor or blender.

2 Measure half a glass of apple juice and add to the fruit. Whiz everything together for a few seconds.

3 Pour into a tall glass and garnish with the leafy stick of celery.

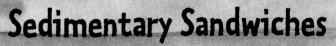
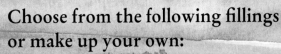

Sedimentary Sandwiches

Build up layers of rock and sediment using all kinds of breads and fillings. About 4 slices of different types of bread and 3 fillings looks very geological!

Try using dark German rye bread, wholemeal and granary slices. See what interesting breads you can find.

Choose from the following fillings or make up your own:

- Slices of cheese
- Cream cheese mixed with chopped black grapes
- Tuna flakes with mayonnaise and chopped cucumber
- Slices of ham, salami or other cold meats
- Hummus or other spreads and dips that you like

1 Cut the crusts off the slices of bread.

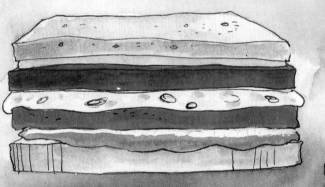

2 Layer the fillings and bread slices until you have built up several layers of sediment.

3 Slice in half and serve.

Fossil Formation

When a dinosaur died its body might sink into a river. The flesh would rot or be eaten by other creatures. The bones would gradually be covered in layers of sand and mud. Over time these sediments would turn into rock and the bones would become as hard as rock too, preserving the skeleton.

Over millions of years the layers of rock are worn away or eroded. Then the dinosaur bones are uncovered and a lucky scientist might discover them!

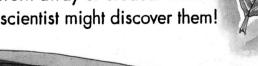

Mammoth Tusks in Mud

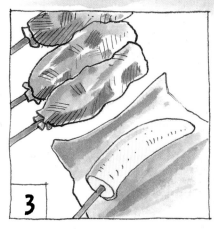

Excavate your own hairy mammoth remains from your freezer. This is some of the tastiest mud you will ever find!

What you will need for the tusks:

- 4 ripe bananas
- 4 wooden skewers, with the points snipped off
- kitchen foil

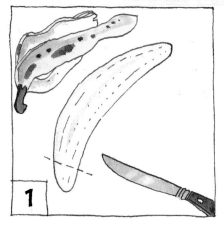

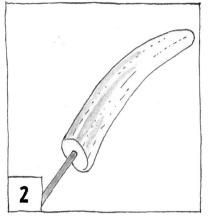

1 Peel the bananas. Cut a little bit off the end of each one. (Eat this!)

2 Push a wooden skewer into the cut end of each banana. Push it as far as you can without it coming through the curved side.

3 Cut 4 pieces of foil and wrap each banana in one. Put in the freezer overnight.

What you will need for the mud:

- 100 g dark chocolate
- 150 ml double cream

1 Break up the chocolate into pieces and place in a small saucepan. Melt it gently, stirring all the time.

2 Add the cream. Whisk it into the chocolate as you heat it gently.

BE CAREFUL AS THE MUD IS VERY HOT!

To serve: Pour the mud into individual bowls.

Take the tusks out of the freezer and unwrap.

Give everyone a tusk each and get stuck into the mud!

Woolly Mammoths

These enormous, hairy, elephant-like creatures lived in the cold regions of Europe, Asia and North America during the last Ice Age. They had giant tusks – the longest fossil tusk found is about 4 metres long – but they were plant-eaters not meat-eaters.

Deep-frozen fossils of woolly mammoths have been found in areas of the world, like Siberia, where the temperature hasn't risen above freezing for hundreds of thousands of years.

Gastroliths

Some plant-eating dinosaurs used to swallow stones and pebbles – known as gastroliths – to help them break up and digest their food. Scientists have found these stones inside the fossilized ribcages of many dinosaur skeletons. Now you can make some!

What you will need to make 15–20 gastroliths:

- 1 tin of chickpeas, drained and rinsed
- 1 clove of garlic, peeled and roughly chopped
- 1½ tablespoons tahini (sesame seed paste)
- 1 egg, beaten
- ½ teaspoon ground cumin
- 75 g breadcrumbs, preferably fresh
- salt and pepper
- pinch of cayenne pepper (optional)

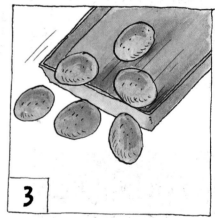

1 Put the chickpeas, garlic, tahini, egg and cumin in a food processor and blend them well.

2 Turn the mixture into a bowl and mix in the breadcrumbs, some salt and pepper, and the cayenne if you like.

3 Form the mixture into small stone shapes and place on a greased baking tray. Bake in the oven at 180°C/350°F/Gas 4 for 15–20 minutes.

Gastrotip
Serve these stones with a squeeze of lemon juice inside some warm pitta bread with salad.

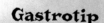

Dino Digestion

Sauropods were plant-eating dinosaurs that could not really chew very well because their jaws didn't move the right way to grind up their food. Some of them, like Diplodocus, had no back teeth at all. They used to swallow branches and leaves whole and that's why they needed the help of stones in their stomachs to digest the stuff. Ow!